WILD NATURE

ENDANGERED ANIMALS

Jinny Johnson

Miles Kelly

First published as *My Top 20 Endangered Animals* in 2010 by Miles Kelly Publishing Ltd
Harding's Barn, Bardfield End Green, Thaxted, Essex, CM6 3PX, UK

This edition published in 2013

10 9 8 7 6 5 4 3 2 1

Publishing Director Belinda Gallagher
Creative Director Jo Cowan
Editorial Director Rosie McGuire
Senior Editor Claire Philip
Concept Designer Simon Lee
Volume Designer Joe Jones, Rob Hale
Image Manager Liberty Newton
Production Manager Elizabeth Collins
Reprographics Stephan Davis, Thom Allaway

ISBN 978-1-78209-097-7

Printed in China

British Library Cataloguing-in-Publication Data
A catalogue record for this book is available from the British Library

ACKNOWLEDGEMENTS
The publishers would like to thank the following sources for the use of their photographs:
Key: (m) = main (i) = inset

Front cover: (main) Khoroshunova Olga/Shutterstock.com, (Wild Nature animal globe) ranker/Shutterstock.com
Back cover: (top) Karen Kane - Alberta, Canada/Shutterstock.com, (bottom) Eric Gevaert/Shutterstock.com
Page 1 Sergey Uryadnikov/Shutterstock.com
Pages 4–5 (clockwise from bottom left) Splashdown Direct/Photolibrary.com, Richard La Val/Photolibrary.com,
Cyril Ruoso/Minden Pictures/FLPA, Gerard Soury/Photolibrary.com, Fritz Poelking/Photolibrary.com
Sumatran rhinoceros (m) Cyril Ruoso/Minden Pictures/FLPA, (i) Cyril Ruoso/Minden Pictures/FLPA
Aye-aye (m) Thomas Marent/Minden Pictures/FLPA, (i) Mark Carwardine/naturepl.com
Przewalski's horse (m) ZSSD/Minden Pictures/FLPA, (i) Eric Baccega/naturepl.com
Saiga antelope (m) Paul Johnson/naturepl.com, (i) Igor Shpilenok/naturepl.com
California condor (m) Michael Durham/Minden Pictures/FLPA, (i) John Cancalosi/naturepl.com
Red panda (m) Juan Carlos Munoz/naturepl.com
Grand cayman blue iguana (m) Jurgen & Christine Sohns/FLPA
Crested ibis (m) Mitsuaki Iwago/Minden Pictures/FLPA, (i) Xi Zhinong/naturepl.com
Hawksbill turtle (m) Reinhard Dirscherl/FLPA, (i) Solvin Zankl/naturepl.com
Galapagos flightless cormorant (m) Tui De Roy/Minden Pictures/FLPA, (i) Pete Oxford/naturepl.com
Kakapo (m) Tui De Roy/Minden Pictures/FLPA, (i) Frans Lanting/FLPA
Mountain gorilla (m) Daniel J. Cox/Photolibrary.com, (i) Thomas Marent/Minden Pictures/FLPA
Black-footed ferret (m) ZSSD/Minden Pictures/FLPA
Asiatic lion (m) Anup Shah/naturepl.com
Orang-utan (m) Berndt Fischer/Photolibrary.com, (i) Anup Shah/naturepl.com
Snow leopard (m) Francois Savigny/naturepl.com, (i) Terry Whittaker/FLPA
Leafy sea dragon (m) Fred Bavendam/Minden Pictures/FLPA, (i) Peter Scoones/naturepl.com
Giant panda (m) Gerry Ellis/Minden Pictures/FLPA, (i) Aflo/naturepl.com
Sea otter (m) Frans Lanting/FLPA (i) Doc White/naturepl.com
Axolotl (m) Jane Burton/naturepl.com

Every effort has been made to acknowledge the source and copyright holder of each picture.
Miles Kelly Publishing apologises for any unintentional errors or omissions.

Made with paper from a sustainable forest

www.mileskelly.net info@mileskelly.net

www.factsforprojects.com

CONTENTS

GOING, GOING... GONE FOREVER

↓ Scientists think the golden toad, which used to live in Costa Rica, is now extinct because of rising temperatures in its forest home.

Some of the most amazing creatures on our planet are struggling for survival. From mighty mammals to tiny insects, many species are in danger of disappearing forever if not enough is done to save them.

Sadly, humans are at the root of many of these problems. We destroy habitats to create space for roads, farms and houses. We kill animals for food, sport and body parts such as fur and horns, and we pollute land, rivers, lakes and oceans, causing untold harm to wildlife.

Fortunately, many organizations are now trying to repair the damage and protect vulnerable animals, and it is hoped that at least some of these measures will succeed.

1

→ Higher temperatures in the Arctic mean less pack ice, so it is getting harder for polar bears to move around and hunt.

GLOBAL WARMING

Average temperatures are increasing and weather conditions in many parts of the globe are changing. This can affect animals' breeding patterns and the availability of food supplies, making life very difficult for some.

KEEP US COOL

2

HABITAT DESTRUCTION

The chopping down of forests and the disturbance of other natural areas is one of the most serious threats to wildlife. If a habitat is destroyed then so are the places in which animals nest and shelter, and the plants they eat.

SAVE MY HOME

↖ The bonobo is now rare and in grave danger of extinction because of hunting and the loss of much of its forest home.

↖ So many hyacinth macaws were captured for sale as pets that the species became very rare. Conservation efforts mean it is now recovering in one area of Brazil.

4

HUNTING

People have always hunted the animals that live close to them, but they only took what they needed for food. However, large-scale commercial hunting kills huge numbers of animals, and drives many species to extinction.

LET ME LIVE

3

DON'T TAKE ME

PET TRADE

Capture of animals for sale as pets has driven some species to extinction. Tragically, for every animal that is sold as a pet, many more die while being illegally smuggled out of their home country.

← After being hunted for hundreds of years, sperm whales are now largely protected. They are still killed accidentally by fishing gear and in collisions with boats.

The smallest and most endangered of the five rhino species, the Sumatran rhinoceros lives in tropical rainforest where it feeds on leaves and fruit. Numbers of this species are now dangerously low and there may be fewer than 250 left in the wild. Thousands of animals have been killed for body parts, which are used in traditional medicine, and although hunting is now illegal, poaching continues. Sumatran rhinos are now being bred in captivity for release into the wild.

MUD WALLOWER

STAR FACT

Rhino horns are made of keratin – the same material as our fingernails. Poachers still hunt rhinos because demand for body parts continues. Horns are sold illegally, and fetch high prices.

SPECIAL FEATURES

HORNS: Males have two horns while some females have only one. Front horns can be 79 cm long. Back horns are usually less than 10 cm.

HAIRY BODY: The hairiest of all rhino species, the Sumatran rhino has tufts of stiff hair all over its tough, leathery skin.

Sumatran rhinoceros

Scientific name: *Dicerorhinus sumatrensis*
Type: Mammal
Lifespan: 30–45 years
Length: 2–3 m
Weight: 600–950 kg
Range: Sumatra, Malaysia, Borneo
Status: Critically endangered

YUMMY...

This rhino is most active after dusk, when it searches for food. It may eat up to 50 kg of plants in a day.

THAT'S BETTER...

During the day the Sumatran rhinoceros enjoys wallowing in ponds or muddy waterholes to keep itself cool and get relief from biting insects. It can swim well.

UPPER LIP: The rhino uses its strong, flexible upper lip to grasp hold of vegetation. Its diet includes fruits, leaves and bark.

SENSES: Its eyesight is poor, but this rhino has keen senses of smell and hearing. It marks its territory with scent trails to let other rhinos know it is there.

One of the strangest of all animals, the aye-aye is a type of lemur. It is related to monkeys, but has bat-like ears and teeth like a rodent. This curious creature lives only on the island of Madagascar. It was believed to be almost extinct, but has since been discovered living in more parts of the island than was previously thought. However its population is still small, and it faces being killed by farmers because it damages crops, and because local people believe it to be an omen of evil.

FREAKY FINGERS

I CAN HEAR YOU...

This strange primate taps on tree trunks or branches and listens intently. If it hears scurrying noises inside it gnaws a hole in the bark and prises out the insects with its extra-long finger.

SPECIAL FEATURES

LONG FINGERS: The third finger on each of the aye-aye's hands is extra-long and very thin, for winkling out insect larvae from beneath bark.

FRONT TEETH: As in rodents, the aye-aye's incisors (front teeth) grow continuously throughout its life. It uses them to chew wood and nuts.

Aye-aye

Scientific name: *Daubentonia madagascariensis*
Type: Mammal
Lifespan: 20 years in captivity
Length: Head-body 36–43 cm, tail up to 60 cm
Weight: Up to 2.5 kg
Range: Madagascar
Status: Near threatened

WAKE UP…

The aye-aye sleeps all day in a nest high in the trees, emerging at dusk to search for food such as insects and their larvae (undeveloped young), seeds and nectar.

EXTRA EYELIDS: Extra, transparent eyelids (nictitating membranes) protect each of the aye-aye's eyes when it is gnawing through wood in search of its insect prey.

LARGE EYES: Its big, yellow-orange eyes help the aye-aye to make the most of any available light as it hunts for food at night.

Once common across the steppes (plains) of Central Asia, Przewalski's horse became extinct in the wild 50 years ago. It suffered from hunting, climate change and competition with livestock (farm animals) introduced into its habitat by people, as well as from some particularly harsh winters when numbers were already low. Some of the last remaining animals were captured and a successful breeding programme has been started.

STEPPE DWELLER

OUCH...

Male Przewalski's horses have fierce fights as they compete against each other to gather females during the breeding season.

SPECIAL FEATURES

STOCKY BODY: Przewalski's horse is smaller than the average domestic horse but has a very strong, muscular body.

STRONG JAWS: Powerful jaws and teeth help these horses to crop the tough plants that grow on the cold, dry steppe.

Przewalski's horse

Scientific name: *Equus ferus przewalski*
Type: Mammal
Lifespan: About 20 years
Length: Head-body 2 m, tail 90 cm
Weight: 350 kg
Range: Mongolia
Status: Critically endangered

'STAR FACT'

There are now more than 300 Przewalski's horses living wild in Mongolia, all descendants of around a dozen animals. They have also been introduced in China, where they are strictly protected.

NEIGH...

Females and their young live in herds led by a dominant male. The mares give birth to one foal after a pregnancy of 11 or 12 months.

THICK COAT: The horse's red-brown coat is short during summer but grows longer and thicker in winter for warmth.

SENSES: Keen senses of hearing and smell alert Przewalski's horse to approaching danger from a great distance away.

Herds of the strange saiga antelope once roamed the grasslands and deserts of Central Asia. Only 20 years ago there were probably around one million saiga, but uncontrolled hunting and a lack of proper protection has caused a dramatic fall in numbers. Now there are fewer than 50,000. Males in particular are hunted because their horns are used in traditional medicine. Greater protection is urgently needed if this species is to survive.

NOSY ROAMER

BATTLE TIME...

Male saigas engage in fierce battles to win as many females as possible during the breeding season, often fighting to the death.

SPECIAL FEATURES

HORNS: Male saigas have a pair of ridged horns, up to 25 cm in length. They use these in battles with rival males during the breeding season.

NOSE: The saiga's strange, long nose has a very special structure, which is thought to help warm air in winter and filter out dust in summer.

'STAR FACT'

During the breeding season, male saigas are so busy fighting and defending their females that they have little time to eat and 90 percent of them may die.

Saiga antelope

Scientific name: *Saiga tatarica*
Type: Mammal
Lifespan: 10–12 years
Length: Head-body up to 1.4 m, tail 6–12 cm
Weight: Male 30–50 kg, female 20–45 kg
Range: Russia, Kazakhstan, western Mongolia
Status: Critically endangered

AMAZING...

The saiga's big, bulbous nose may help it to control its body temperature by cooling or warming its blood as necessary.

WOOLLY FUR: In winter the saiga's coat thickens and grows a long fringe on the chest, helping to keep the animal warm. In summer it moults, becoming quite sparse.

FAST RUNNER: The saiga can run at speeds of up to 80 km/h for long distances as it roams the grasslands in search of food.

The magnificent California condor is one of the world's most endangered birds. In 1981 there were only 22 left in the wild, and a few years later the last six were captured to start a captive breeding programme. A number of captive-bred California condors have now been released into the wild in California and Mexico and some have even hatched chicks. One of the main problems the condor faces is lead poisoning – many die after eating the carcasses of animals that have been killed by hunters using lead shot.

SUPER GLIDER

AWESOME...

Each condor released into the wild is carefully monitored. Tags and radio transmitters on the huge wings help scientists to track and identify individuals.

STAR FACT

This species was virtually extinct 30 years ago, but there are now nearly 300 California condors living in the wild, thanks to conservation measures.

SPECIAL FEATURES

KEEN EYESIGHT: Sharp eyes let the condor spot food on the ground from great heights as it soars over plains and mountains.

STRONG BEAK: The large and powerful beak has a sharply hooked tip, which helps the bird to rip apart its prey.

California condor

Scientific name: *Gymnogyps californianus*
Type: Bird
Lifespan: Up to 60 years
Length: 1.1–1.4 m
Weight: Up to 8.8 kg
Range: Western North America –
   California and Mexico
Status: Critically endangered

The condor is a member of the New World vulture family. Like others of its kind it has bare skin on its head, so it can stick its head into rotting flesh without getting blood and gore all over its feathers.

PRETTY UGLY...

LONG WINGS: With a wingspan of 2.9 m, the condor can glide high above the ground on warm air currents, only needing to beat its wings occasionally.

FEET: The condor's feet are used for walking rather than killing prey so it has short claws instead of long talons like some birds of prey.

The beautiful red panda lives in mountain bamboo forests. Like the giant panda, it feeds mainly on bamboo, as well as other plants, nuts and eggs. Many forests in the region have been cleared to create space for farming, livestock and timber, so numbers of red pandas have fallen dramatically. Although they are protected, they continue to be killed by poachers for their fine fur, which even covers the soles of their feet.

COSY CLIMBER

STAR FACT

Scientists have long argued about exactly what kind of animal the red panda is. It is not a bear like its namesake, the giant panda, and most now agree that it is a kind of raccoon.

Red panda

Scientific name: Ailurus fulgens
Type: Mammal
Lifespan: 8–10 years
Length: Head-body 51–63 cm, tail up to 48 cm
Weight: 3–6 kg
Range: Western China and eastern Himalayas
Status: Vulnerable

CHOMP...

Red pandas spend more than half of every day feeding. Bamboo is not a very nourishing food so they need to eat lots of it in order to survive.

SPECIAL FEATURES

TAIL: Its long, bushy tail helps the red panda to balance when climbing, as well as providing extra warmth on cold nights.

SPECIAL WRIST BONE: Like giant pandas, the red panda has two extended wrist bones. It uses them like thumbs to help it grip its food.

GIANT LIZARD

This striking plant-eating iguana is one of the rarest of all lizards. It has been killed by dogs and cats introduced to its island home, and much of its habitat and food supply have been lost as fruit farms have been felled to make grazing land for cattle. In 2002 there were probably fewer than 25 blue iguanas left in the wild. They are now being reared in captivity and some have been released in protected areas.

Grand Cayman blue iguana

Scientific name: *Cyclura lewisi*
Type: Lizard
Lifespan: Possibly 60 years or more
Length: 1.5 m
Weight: 11 kg
Range: Grand Cayman Island
Status: Critically endangered

COOL...

Normally greyish-blue in colour, this lizard turns bright blue during the breeding season – the male goes a deeper shade than the female.

STAR FACT

The female blue iguana is a caring mum. She digs a nest in the soil in which to lay her eggs. Then she covers the nest to hide it from predators and guards the site until they hatch.

SPECIAL FEATURES

TOES: Its jointed toes help the iguana when digging nests in the ground and climbing – it can climb to 5 m in trees.

EYESIGHT: This iguana has good eyesight and can see shapes and movement over long distances. It does not see well at night.

The extremely rare crested ibis has a long, downward-curving beak, a bright red face and a crest of feathers on the back of its head. One of the main problems this distinctive bird faces has been the loss of feeding areas. It feeds mostly on fish and other creatures living in rice paddies (fields filled with water in which rice is grown) and other wetlands, and many of these areas have been converted to wheat farms. The ibis also used to be killed by hunters but is now officially protected.

CRESTED WADER

DINNER TIME...

The female lays up to five eggs, which her mate helps to incubate (keep warm). Once they hatch, both parents are busy fetching food for their hungry brood.

SPECIAL FEATURES

BEAK: The long, slender, downward-curving beak is ideal for probing in muddy water to find fish, frogs and other food.

LONG LEGS: Like many waterbirds, the crested ibis has long legs so it can paddle through water or wetlands without getting its body wet.

Crested ibis

Scientific name: *Nipponia nippon*
Type: Bird
Lifespan: About 20 years
Length: 75 cm (including tail)
Weight: 1 kg
Range: China, Japan and eastern Russia (now extinct in some areas)
Status: Endangered

SNAP...

A crested ibis snatches an insect from the air in its long beak. Although the ibis has white feathers for much of the year, its plumage turns grey during the breeding season.

STAR FACT

In 1981 only about seven of these spectacular birds were known to remain in the wild. Thanks to protective measures there are now thought to be as many as 500, and captive-bred birds have been released in Japan.

COLOURFUL HEAD: The skin on the ibis' head is bare of feathers and bright red in colour, and its beak is also tipped with red.

CREST: Both male and female birds of this species have a crest of feathers at the back of the head, which they raise during courtship displays.

One of the smaller sea turtles, the hawksbill has the most beautiful shell, which, sadly, is one reason for its rarity. Millions have been killed for their shells, which are used to make jewellery and other items, and although they are now protected, trade continues. Like all turtles, the hawksbill also suffers from the loss of nesting sites as coastal areas are built on. They are also killed for their meat, their eggs are taken and many are caught in nets or damaged by oil spills.

SPECTACULAR SHELL

GET A MOVE ON...

Hawksbills lay their eggs on land. When the babies hatch they have to scuttle down the beach to the sea as fast as they can before they get caught by predators such as crabs and seabirds.

SPECIAL FEATURES

FLIPPER-LIKE LIMBS: The hawksbill's legs have evolved into flippers, which it uses to push itself strongly through the water.

BEAK-LIKE JAWS: Its narrow, hooked beak allows the turtle to lever food such as sponges and sea anemones from crevices in coral reefs.

Hawksbill turtle

Scientific name: *Eretmochelys imbricata*
Type: Reptile
Lifespan: 30–50 years
Length: Up to 91 cm
Weight: Up to 136 kg
Range: Tropical and subtropical waters of the Atlantic, Pacific and Indian oceans
Status: Critically endangered

TASTY...

Sponges are the hawksbill's main food but it also eats molluscs, sea urchins, fish and jellyfish.

STAR FACT

Although marine turtles are expert swimmers and spend nearly all their lives in the ocean, only coming to shore to breed, they breathe air and must surface regularly.

CLAWS: There are two claws on each of the hawksbill's front flippers. Most marine turtles have only one claw on each.

SHELL: Its heavy shell is strikingly patterned in amber, yellow or brown, and is covered with thick, overlapping bony plates

The only flightless cormorant, this extraordinary bird evolved on islands, where there were no land predators. It hunts in the ocean and had no need to fly, but when humans came to the islands they brought animals such as cats, dogs and rats, which destroyed many birds and their eggs. Many have also been caught in fishing nets. As a result, the flightless cormorant has become one of the world's rarest birds. It now lives on only two of the Galapagos Islands and numbers are carefully monitored.

FLIGHTLESS FISHER

Both parents help to incubate the clutch of three eggs and feed the chicks once they hatch.

SIT TIGHT...

'STAR FACT

Pairs of these cormorants give each other presents. When one parent arrives back at the nest it brings an offering of seaweed for the sitting bird, which might otherwise drive its mate away.

SPECIAL FEATURES

FEET: Webbed feet and strong legs help this cormorant to speed through the water as it searches for fish and other food.

HOOKED BEAK: Long, strong and sharp-tipped, the beak is ideally shaped for grasping and holding onto the bird's slippery prey.

Galapagos flightless cormorant

Scientific name: *Phalacrocorax harrisi*
Type: Bird
Lifespan: Up to 50 years
Length: 90–100 cm
Weight: 4 kg
Range: Galapagos Islands
Status: Endangered

FLAP...

A cormorant holds its stumpy wings out to dry in the sun. The wings, like those of all cormorants, are not waterproof so the bird must allow them to dry after a fishing trip.

SMALL WINGS: This cormorant doesn't use its wings for swimming or flying, but it does hold them out for balance as it clambers over rocks on the shoreline.

QUICK BREEDER: Females can lay several clutches of eggs each year, which may help this species to survive in spite of the threats it faces.

One of the world's strangest birds, the kakapo is a type of parrot. It is the heaviest parrot, the only one that is nocturnal and the only one that cannot fly. It was common in New Zealand, where there were no land predators, until humans arrived bringing animals such as cats, dogs and rats. By 1976 only about 18 birds remained. Now, thanks to strict protection and captive breeding there are as many 124 birds, but the kakapo needs continued help if it is to survive.

NIGHT PARROT

'STAR FACT

Unusually among birds, the kakapo has a very good sense of smell, which helps it to find food. Unfortunately, it also has a strong smell itself, making it easy for predators to find.

CRUNCH...

The kakapo feeds mostly on plant foods such as berries, seeds, fruit, leaves and flowers.

SPECIAL FEATURES

CAMOUFLAGE: Beautiful mossy-green feathers, mottled with brown and yellow, help the kakapo to stay hidden on the ground.

STRONG LEGS: The kakapo cannot fly but it can run fast on its strong, sturdy legs and can even climb trees.

Kakapo

Scientific name: *Strigops habroptilus*
Type: Bird
Lifespan: Possibly up to 90 years
Length: 60 cm
Weight: 3.5 kg
Range: New Zealand
Status: Critically endangered

I'M OVER HERE...

In the breeding season, the male kakapo makes a loud booming call to attract females. The sound can be heard from several kilometres away.

WINGS: Although this bird is flightless, its wings are still useful. The kakapo holds them out when running, which helps it to balance.

WHISKERS: Highly sensitive, whisker-like feathers around its beak help the kakapo to find its way at night as it walks along with its head lowered.

Largest of all primates, the gorilla is a peaceful creature that lives on plant food and spends its time resting, feeding and playing. Tragically these highly intelligent animals are now increasingly rare, having suffered from habitat loss and from poachers, who kill them for meat and to sell body parts as souvenirs. Poachers also take young for the illegal pet trade and kill the rest of the family. War and unrest in their home region has also affected the gorillas, and makes it harder to protect them.

GENTLE GIANT

MUNCH...

A male gorilla may eat as much as 30 kg of plant food, such as leaves, flowers, roots and fruit, every day. That's like eating 30 lettuces and 50 apples!

CLEAR OFF...

A gorilla family is led by a dominant male, often known as a silverback because of the pale hair he develops on his back upon reaching maturity. He will protect his family from intruders if necessary.

SPECIAL FEATURES

WARM FUR: This species has longer fur than its lowland relative to protect it from the cold and damp of its mountain home.

HUGE STRENGTH: A male gorilla can weigh at least three times as much as an adult man and has the strength of six or more.

Mountain gorilla

Scientific name: *Gorilla beringei beringei*
Type: Mammal
Lifespan: About 35 years
Height: Males up to 1.8 m, females 1.5 m
Weight: Males up to 210 kg, females 115 kg
Range: Virunga mountains in Rwanda, Uganda and the Democratic Republic of Congo
Status: Endangered

'STAR FACT

Figures from the World Wildlife Fund (WWF) suggest that there has been a small increase in the population of wild mountain gorillas and that there may be about 700 animals.

HANDS AND FEET: Like us, gorillas have opposable thumbs, so they can grip and manipulate things with great skill. They have opposable toes too!

STRONG TEETH: A gorilla has 32 teeth, including pointed incisors for biting off leaves and large, flat molars for chewing tough plant food.

Around 100 years ago there were thousands of these sharp-toothed predators on the plains of North America. But by 1987 the black-footed ferret was extinct in the wild. One reason was that its main prey, prairie dogs, were wiped out from much of their former range because they damaged farmland. The ferrets are now being bred in captivity and reintroduced into the wild. If they are to survive, prairie dog numbers must also recover.

PRAIRIE PREDATOR

Black-footed ferret

Scientific name: Mustela nigripes
Type: Mammal
Lifespan: 3–4 years
Length: Head-body 38–50 cm, tail 11–13 cm
Weight: Up to 1 kg
Range: North America
Status: Endangered

READY...

A wily hunter, the colour and markings of this ferret's fur help it to blend well with its prairie surroundings, making it hard to spot until it moves.

'STAR FACT'

Black-footed ferret numbers are on the increase. Every year about 200 young animals are being released into the wild in locations in eight western US states and in Mexico.

SPECIAL FEATURES

STRONG CLAWS: The ferret uses its large front paws and strong claws for digging its way into prairie dog burrows.

SLENDER BODY: The ferret's long, slender body allows it to slip into narrow burrows in pursuit of its prey.

FOREST HUNTER

As recently as 200 years ago, Asiatic lions ranged over a large area from Greece through the Middle East to India. Sadly, most were killed by hunters in the 19th century and there are now probably only around 300 in the wild, all in the protected Gir Forest area of western India. Closely related to the African lion, the Asiatic lion is slightly smaller and lives in smaller prides. They are now protected, but some are still killed by poachers.

ROAR...

Like all big cats, the Asiatic lion is a powerful hunter. Its main prey are the chital and sambar deer but it also hunts wild boar, antelope and water buffalo.

Asiatic lion

Scientific name: *Panthera leo persica*
Type: Mammal
Lifespan: 16–18 years
Length: Head-body up to 2.5 m, tail 70–105 cm
Weight: Male 150–250 kg, female 120–180 kg
Range: Gujerat State, India
Status: Endangered

STAR FACT

There are plans to establish a second population of Asiatic lions in the Kuno Wildlife Sanctuary, Madhya Pradesh (central India). Just one population means that they are currently very vulnerable.

SPECIAL FEATURES

MANE: The manes of male Asiatic lions are shorter and less luxuriant than those of their African cousins, and their tail tufts are longer.

BELLY FOLD: All Asiatic lions have an obvious fold of skin running along the belly. African lions do not have this.

The name 'orang-utan' means 'man of the forest', and this primate is the largest of all tree-living animals. An agile climber, it swings easily between trees as it searches for fruit and other food. Orang-utans are now seriously endangered, mainly because of the destruction of their habitat, and may become extinct in the next 20 years. Young animals are sometimes caught by poachers and sold as pets. A number of centres are working to protect orang-utans and look after orphaned and injured animals.

KING OF SWING

STRETCH...

The orang-utan swings easily from branch to branch using its long arms and can also walk along branches, holding on with its strong feet.

'STAR FACT'

Orang-utans use simple tools. They hold large leaves over themselves as shelter, and use sticks to scratch themselves, reach fruit at the end of branches, or extract insects from holes.

SPECIAL FEATURES

LONG ARMS: These help the orang-utan get around the forest canopy with ease and hang upside down from branches when feeding.

THUMBS: Like humans, orang-utans have opposable thumbs. They also have opposable big toes, so they can grip objects well with their feet.

Orang-utan

Scientific name: *Pongo pygmaeus*
(Borneo orang-utan); *Pongo abelii*
(Sumatran orang-utan)
Type: Mammal
Lifespan: 45–50 years
Length: Up to 1.5 m
Weight: Male 70–130 kg,
female 30–55 kg
Range: Sumatra and Borneo
Status: Endangered (*P. pygmaeus*):
Critically endangered (*P. abelii*)

SNOOZE...

An orang-utan spends most of its life high in the trees, and makes a nest from branches to sleep in each night. They are generally solitary, except when caring for young.

LARGE CHEEK PADS: Around the age of 15, a male orang-utan develops large cheek pads. These show females that he is ready for breeding.

HAIR: Both species of orang-utan have distinctive coats of long, coarse, reddish-brown hair covering the body, but the face is always bare.

The beautiful snow leopard lives in remote mountain areas and is rarely seen. There may only be 3500 to 7000 of these magnificent animals left in the wild. For years these leopards were hunted for their fur and also for body parts, for use in traditional medicine. They are now protected but poaching continues, and they are suffering from habitat loss and falling numbers of their prey. The leopards may also be shot by people who want to prevent them killing cattle.

COOL CAT

CUTE CUBS...

Females give birth to two or three cubs in late spring. The cubs stay with their mother for nearly two years.

STAR FACT

Unlike most big cats, the snow leopard can't roar or purr, but it can hiss, growl and make a huffing, puffing sound. During the mating season leopards call to each other with loud wails.

SPECIAL FEATURES

TAIL: A long tail helps the snow leopard to balance as it leaps around its mountain home. It also wraps its tail around itself for warmth.

LARGE PAWS: Its big, furry paws act like snow shoes, spreading the leopard's weight to make it easier to walk on snow.

Snow leopard

Scientific name: *Panthera uncia*
Type: Mammal
Lifespan: 15–18 years
Length: Head-body 1.5 m, tail up to 91 cm
Weight: Up to 55 kg
Range: Mountains of Central Asia
Status: Endangered

WATCH OUT...

The snow leopard is a solitary hunter. It stalks prey animals such as wild goats, getting as close as it can before the final pounce. It can jump 15 m in a single bound.

SPECIALIZED LUNGS: Extra-large lungs help the snow leopard to survive at high altitudes where oxygen levels are low.

COAT: The smoky-grey markings on the snow leopard's coat make it hard to see in its rocky home and help it remain unnoticed when stalking prey.

Looking more like a plant than a fish, the extraordinary camouflage of the leafy sea dragon makes it hard to spot as it lurks among floating seaweed. These little creatures have become rare due to the loss and disruption of many areas of seaweed, leaving them with fewer places to hide and find food. Some are also accidentally caught in nets and in the past divers have captured them to keep as pets. Leafy sea dragons are now protected and cannot be removed from the sea.

WEEDY WONDER

WOW...

Once the female sea dragon has laid her eggs, the male carries them on the underside of his tail until they hatch. Here you can see the clusters of tiny eggs waiting to hatch into sea dragons.

LOOK AGAIN...

The branching tendrils of the leafy sea dragon's strange body provide a brilliant disguise as it hovers among strands of seaweed.

SPECIAL FEATURES

LONG SNOUT: The sea dragon sucks up its food – tiny sea creatures – with it long snout and small mouth.

FINS: Small fins on its back and sides allow the sea dragon to move through the water, but it is not a strong swimmer.

Leafy sea dragon

Scientific name: *Phydodurus eques*
Type: Fish
Lifespan: Up to 10 years in captivity
Length: Up to 35 cm
Range: Coastal waters of south and east Australia
Status: Near threatened

STAR FACT

A leafy sea dragon's eyes can move independently of each other. One eye can be looking one way while the other eye looks another – useful when watching out for enemies.

LEAFY FLAPS: Many delicate flaps on the sea dragon's body help it to hide from the watchful eyes of predators in its plant-filled habitat.

SPINES: The sea dragon has some sharp spines on the sides of its body, which it may use to defend itself against attackers, such as predatory fish.

The best known of all endangered animals, the giant panda is still struggling for survival. Huge efforts have been made to protect this large, shy bear, and it is thought that the population has increased. Pandas live in the mountain forests of China and feed mainly on bamboo, so the destruction of bamboo forests has been its greatest threat. Poaching used to be more of a problem but the giant panda is now strictly protected so this threat has been reduced.

RAREST BEAR

EAT UP...

Bamboo leaves, stems and shoots are the panda's main food. This diet isn't very filling so the panda needs to eat as much as 30 kg a day to get enough nourishment.

LOOK AT ME...

Pandas are good climbers from a young age and can also swim well when necessary.

SPECIAL FEATURES

TEETH AND JAWS: Broad, flat teeth and strong jaw muscles are ideally suited to crunching and grinding tough bamboo stems and shoots.

WRIST BONE: An enlarged wrist bone on each front foot acts like an opposable thumb to help the panda grip its food.

Giant panda

Scientific name: *Ailuropoda melanoleuca*
Type: Mammal
Lifespan: 14–20 years
Length: Head-body 1.5 m, tail 10–15 cm
Weight: 100–150 kg
Range: Southwest China
Status: Endangered

'STAR FACT'

Most giant pandas now live in protected reserves. There are more than 50 such reserves, and they cover an area of more than 2.5 million acres.

SENSE OF SMELL: The panda's excellent sense of smell helps it avoid other pandas for most of the year, and then find mates in the breeding season.

THICK FUR: Very thick, coarse, oily fur helps to keep the panda warm and dry in its cold, wet home in the mountains of western China.

Sea otters spend most of their lives in the water. They dive to depths of up to 75 metres to find mussels and clams to eat, but their thick fur keeps them warm. They are one of the few animals to use tools, breaking open their shelled prey with rocks. Sea otters are threatened by oil spills, as oil damages their fur and causes harm if swallowed. Many also die in fishing nets, or have been killed by an infectious disease. Some sea otters have been bred in captivity and released into the wild to boost numbers.

TOOL USER

RELAX...

Sea otters rest in the water, lying on their backs among kelp (a kind of giant seaweed). They sometimes wrap themselves up in the kelp so they aren't swept away by ocean currents.

SPECIAL FEATURES

BACK FEET: Its large, webbed back feet act like flippers, helping the sea otter to power through the water.

FRONT FEET: The small front paws have claws that can be retracted (withdrawn inside the paws). These are used for holding food and grooming.

Sea otter

Scientific name: *Enhydra lutris*
Type: Mammal
Lifespan: 15–20 years
Length: Head-body 1.2 m,
    tail up to 37 cm
Weight: Male 22–45 kg,
    female 15–32 kg
Range: Northern Pacific
    coastal waters
Status: Endangered

GOTCHA...

Sea otters catch fish and squid as well as shellfish. They have big appetites and can eat as much as 30 percent of their body weight in a day.

STAR FACT

The sea otter has the thickest fur of any mammal. There are two layers, called guard hairs and underhairs, and there are as many as 165,000 hairs per square centimetre on some areas of the body.

TEETH: Most of the 32 teeth are broad and flat for crushing shells, but the otter also has four sharp incisors in its lower jaw for scraping flesh from shellfish.

NOSTRILS AND EARS: When the sea otter dives, special flaps close off its nostrils and ears, keeping water out.

The axolotl is a type of salamander. This odd creature keeps some of its larval (immature) features, never developing to true maturity. Axolotls are now so rare they are found in only one lake in Mexico. They have suffered from the draining and pollution of their habitat, and from the introduction of big fish, which compete with the axolotls for food. Many have been captured for the pet trade, and for food – roasted axolotl was a great local delicacy.

FEATHER GILLS

Axolotl

Scientific name: *Ambystoma mexicanum*
Type: Amphibian
Lifespan: 10–15 years
Length: Up to 30 cm
Weight: Up to 227 g
Range: Lake Xochimilco, Mexico
Status: Critically endangered

STRANGE...

Some axolotls are black or brown, but albino, or white, animals are also common.

STAR FACT

Axolotls have an amazing ability – they can regrow body parts if necessary. This feature has long fascinated scientists, who hope to find out how the animals do this.

SPECIAL FEATURES

GILLS: Feathery gills allow the axolotl to breathe in water. All young amphibians have gills like these but most lose them as they develop.

SENSE OF SMELL: The axolotl uses its good sense of smell to help it find food such as worms, insects and small fish.